THESE SACRED DAYS

These Sacred Days

*Walking with Jesus
through the Sacred Triduum*

Brother Richard Contino, OSF

ST PAULS

Library of Congress Cataloging-in-Publication Data

Contino, Richard.
  These sacred days: walking with Jesus through the sacred triduum
/ Richard Contino.
      p. cm.
    ISBN-13: 978-0-8189-1275-7
    ISBN-10: 0-8189-1275-8
    1. Jesus Christ—Passion—Meditations.   I. Title.
    BT431.3.C66 2008
    232.96—dc22

                              2008031110

Produced and designed in the United States of America by the
Fathers and Brothers of the Society of St. Paul,
2187 Victory Boulevard, Staten Island, New York 10314-6603
as part of their communications apostolate.

ISBN-10: 0-8189-1275-8
ISBN-13: 978-0-8189-1275-7

Printing Information:

Current Printing - first digit   1   2   3   4   5   6   7   8   9   10

Year of Current Printing - first year shown

2009 2010 2011 2012 2013 2014 2015 2016 2017 2018

Contents

v

In the Garden

The night was calm.
There was hardly a breeze stirring
   as the band of men made their way
   through the streets of the sleeping city.
Under the moonlit canopy of the night sky
   the city of David –
   Jerusalem –
   glistened and shone brightly.

The group of men
   walked slowly to their destination
   just outside the city.

The Passover meal was over
   yet each man was lost in thought.

"One of you will betray Me!"

The phrase still haunted the group
   as they traveled out beyond the gate
     into the hills surrounding the city.

Who could betray the Master?

Why?

There was a traitor in this sacred group.

This night
   He, the teacher,
      had knelt and washed their feet.

"What I have done for you
   you must do for one another."

Wash the feet of those who are sinners!
   Wash the feet of those who are lonely!
Wash the feet of those who are poor!
   Wash the feet of those who suffer!

"Love one another
   as I have loved you.
If you do so
   they will know you belong to Me."

The Passover meal was like no other.
He took bread,
   blessed and broke it, saying,
      "This is My Body."
Then He took the cup,
   and blessed it saying,
      "This is the cup of My Blood,
         a New Covenant for all.
         Do this in memory of Me."

In the midst of our celebration
   there is profound sadness
      for one of us will betray the Master!

Betrayal!
   Why would anyone betray Jesus? –
Would you?
   Could you?
What price would it take to betray God?

Would you betray God for
   Money?
   Fame?
   Pleasure?
   Power?

Judas did so for thirty pieces of silver.
   Where are those thirty pieces now?
Perhaps they were melted down
   to make rings or earrings!

Maybe down through the centuries
   these coins made their way
   into the pockets of believers
   and non-believers alike.

Strange!
For I am somehow under the impression
   that these silver coins were –
      in a time since past –
   melted and refined and molded

into a chalice that is used at Mass....
How fitting, how appropriate,
that the silver given to betray
holds the Blood that saves!

Jesus,
remember me,
when you come into your Kingdom.

Betrayal is a harsh word,
an ugly deed!

Did Judas not see Jesus
heal the sick
give sight to the blind
free the burden of sinners
touch and embrace the untouchable?

Jesus,
remember me,
when you come into your Kingdom.

Judas had witnessed
Lazarus raised from the dead.
Yet he betrays!

They called Jesus
King and Messiah!
Judas was there.
He saw the crowds;
he heard the acclaim.
Yet he betrays!

Does not Jesus touch our lives?
    forgiving,
    healing,
    loving?
And like Judas
    do not our hands
    grasp and clutch
    at thirty pieces of silver?

Jesus,
    remember me,
    when you come into your Kingdom.

The small band of men,
    led by the Master,
        enters the Garden.

It has been a long night
    and all are exhausted;
        all are nervous and anxious.

Some of the Apostles
    find a spot and settle down
        for a little rest.

They have been here before
    but tonight it all seems so strange.
Jesus, too, is exhausted and looking haggard.
    His normally calm face
        is marked with deep concern.
    His eyes are almost glazed.

Jesus calls Peter, James and John
  to follow Him to a different part
    of the Garden.

"Watch and pray with Me
  as I go over there and pray."

As soon as Jesus leaves
  the trio falls sound asleep.

Jesus is alone!

We are asked to keep watch and pray.
  Did you pray today?
"Can you not keep watch with Me for one hour?"
  Did you attend the Eucharist with heart
    and soul?
Watch and pray!
  Did you hear Sunday's Gospel?
Watch and pray!
  Did you become Eucharist
    for your neighbor?
    and for strangers?
Watch and pray!
  Did you proclaim the Good News this week?
Watch and pray!

When a neighbor needed you –
  Were you sound asleep?
When injustice flourished -
  Were you sound asleep?

When the voiceless needed your voice –
　　Were you sound asleep?
When the hungry asked for food –
　　Were you sound asleep?
When the thirsty yearned for drink –
　　Were you sound asleep?
When the homeless needed shelter –
　　Were you sound asleep?
When the ill were left alone –
　　Were you sound asleep?
When the prisoner and the oppressed needed you –
　　Were you sound asleep?

Watch and pray!
　　Stay awake and be on guard.
Watch and pray!

At a distance Jesus kneels;
　　within seconds He is racked with pain
　　　　and sobbing.
His head,
　　soon to be crowned with thorns,
　　　　is bent.
Tears stream down His cheeks.
　　He knows what awaits Him
　　　　and His body shudders.

Almost like a cry
　　addressed to the now silent heavens,
　　　　"Father, if there is another way.…"

His mind races with images
of rejection, betrayal and denial.
He knows! His mind sees!

Again the cry!
"Father, if there is another way...."
The images now crowd His thoughts:
the beating, the crowning,
the cross, the nails.
He knows! His mind sees!

Then almost as a plea...
"Father, if there is another way."

Jesus,
remember me,
when you come into your Kingdom.

The mission has come down to the final hours;
His ministry is done.

The multitudes are gone.
There will be but one miracle tonight.
There will be no sermons in the Garden.

Elsewhere in the city
Roman and Temple guards are gathering
and collecting their weapons.

Caiaphas, Annas and Pilate
are in consultation.
This must be done under cover of darkness.

The arrest, the trial and the sentence
   carried out in the utmost secrecy
   and accomplished before dawn.

What have we done or failed to do
   that must be covered by the mantle of darkness?
Remember:
   All will be brought into the light.
What secrets do we harbor and keep hidden
   from ourselves,
   from others,
   and from God,
      our Way, our Truth, our Life?

Jesus,
   remember me,
   when you come into your Kingdom.

This is the hour of darkness;
   the forces of evil conspire.
Satan enters the heart of an Apostle,
   the trap is set,
   the plan conceived –
   the powers of darkness gather in this night.

Judas stands by idly
   caressing the pouch of silver.

"You there!" (talking to Judas)
   "Lead my men to seek and arrest this Jesus."
"Me? Lead you?
   No! I gave you the information –

Surely that's enough!"
"No," yells the captain,
   "You have been paid to see this through.
      Now move!"

"This is not what I had bargained for.
   I will consort with evil,
   I will use evil for my own means,
      but to be publicly associated
      with the powers of evil –
      for Jesus to know the truth.…
   I cannot bear that shame.
      Jesus will know.
      The Apostles will see me."

"Lead my men.… Now!"

Jesus,
   remember me,
   when you come into your Kingdom.

The band of guards moved swiftly
   through the quiet streets.
The sound of boots
   hitting the pavement could be heard
      along with the clanking of swords.

Jesus,
   remember me,
   when you come into your Kingdom.

As Judas leads armed men
to capture the Prince of Peace,
consider whether your life
leads others to Christ
or away from Him.

What captures your passions?
The Word?
The Eucharist?
Charity?
Justice?
Hope?

The sound of leather to pavement
echoes in the city streets.
Judas marches at the head.
What must be going through his mind?
He has to face Jesus
and look directly into the Master's eyes.

Jesus,
remember me,
when you come into your Kingdom.

For three years
Judas journeyed with the Christ,
saw Him heal,
heard Him teach,
and even raise the dead.

O ye of little faith!

Jesus is prostrate in the Garden
    weeping, sweating and bleeding,
    about to experience a broken heart.

Jesus trusted, loved and challenged Judas.
    Judas could not reach the bar –
        but that was alright.
Jesus loved him
    in spite of the fact
        that he would not live up
    to the standard Jesus would set
        for him,
        for His Apostles
        and for us.

Judas held the communal pouch.
    He chose his treasures *here*
        instead of storing them up in Heaven
            as Jesus taught.

Judas, the Lord loved you.
    Judas, Jesus chose you.

Jesus has chosen each one of us
    and called each of us by name.
What is in our money pouch?
    Where have we stored our treasure?

Jesus,
    remember me,
    when you come into your Kingdom.

The hour of darkness approaches.
    Jesus meets evil and treachery head on.
Through prayer, He is ready
        to do the Father's will.
    The calm of the Garden
      is broken by violence.
    The peace of our world is shattered
      by hatred,
      intolerance,
      fear
      and greed.
There have been too many deaths
    in the name of peace
    in the name of God,
    Yahweh,
    Father
    or Allah!

This night, however, is different.
    In it
        violence will meet Peace
        shouts will meet Silence
        fear will meet Courage
        death will meet Life
        and evil will meet Good!

Jesus,
    remember me,
    when you come into your Kingdom.

The kiss was planned
    and executed without emotion.
        It stung like a slap.
        It bruised the cheek.
        It was excruciatingly painful.
The words that Judas used
    were like a knife
    aimed and plunged into the heart.

"Do you betray Me, Judas, with a Kiss?"

Jesus is drained of strength
    but resigned.
His eyes are fixed on Judas
    who casts his eyes downward.
        He cannot look at Christ.
The thirty pieces of silver
    in a pouch by his side
        is weighing him down.

Judas flees
    pursued by the demons
        of his heart and mind:
            chaos, confusion, mayhem!
Amidst the yelling, screaming, shouting.
    Jesus remains calm.

And then the soldiers seize their prey.

A sword is drawn
    a blow is struck

a servant stumbles
    and falls to the ground bleeding.
Jesus looks and demands,
    "Put away your swords."
He bends down over the injured man
    and He heals him
        in full view of all in the Garden.

Evil will not be swayed by a miracle.
    It will not be silenced.
    It will not yield –
        not on this night,
        not now.

The forces are gathered.
    The mob becomes real.
Evil and its shadow
    casts its form and cloak of darkness.
For a time that darkness will prevail.
    The Christ is overpowered by the mob,
        treated without dignity,
        without respect.

The Apostles, seized by fear, flee.
    The wolves have attacked the sheepfold.
And the Shepherd
    who is guarding His little flock,
        is attacked and brought down.
Panic invades the flock
    and they all run.

Jesus,
    remember me,
    when you come into your Kingdom.

Alone,
    the Shepherd is bound and led away.
And you can hear evil laughing
    for God has been captured,
    love will be violated,
    mercy and compassion will be imprisoned.

On this night
    heaven is silent and quiet.
The hosts of heaven gaze upon the scene
    and — for the first time —
    there are tears in Heaven.

Jesus,
    remember me,
    when you come into your Kingdom.

The slumbering city rests
    unaware of the powers unleashed.
Jesus, the Lord,
    bound and rudely treated
    is marched to the house of Annas.

Lord, how often you wish to lead us…
    but we resist.
You, instead, allow yourself to be taken
    because it is the Father's will.

Teach us to always seek His will
in trust, and confidence and surrender.

Jesus,
remember me,
when you come into your Kingdom.

They have all fled.
The Apostles ran.
They were not just frightened,
they were scared for their very lives.
These men – called by Jesus –
left Him alone.
The Good Shepherd, however,
did protect those who were His own.
They were unharmed – but, Oh, so fearful.

Some fled back to the safety
of the Upper Room,
bolting the door
and hiding in a corner
of that room
where so much was said
just hours ago.
So much had happened since.
The table is still filled
with the remnants of the meal.
The bowl and the pitcher that
Jesus had used to wash their feet
was still in the center of the room.

So much had changed.
So much was different now.
These men will never be the same again.
The world, this night,
has been changed forever.

Jesus,
remember me,
when you come into your Kingdom.

The Trial Begins

The band of Roman and Temple guards
   snake their way
   through the streets of the city.
They do not wish to call attention
   to themselves
   or to the bound Prisoner in their midst.

The cover of night envelops them.

Satan is delighted on this night
   for, in his grasp,
      he possess the Man
         who would save the world.
Satan may be the great deceiver
   but the Man is the despoiler
      of his plans.

Tonight
   the angels look down
      from Heaven's lofty heights
   and gaze forlorn upon the scene.
Heaven is quiet

for not even its usual praise
    is sung this night to God Most High.

Meanwhile,
    in the caverns of Hell,
        demons and the damned
            are dancing with delight
    for their master is in command
        and the Son is in his grasp.

Jesus,
    remember me,
    when you come into your Kingdom.

The bound Man enters a gate
    escorted through the courtyard
    through an arch and into a chamber.

Lights have been lit…
    men are anxiously awaiting
        the arrival of their captive.
In the midst of the assembly
    stands an older man.
With a determined look,
    he turns his gaze
        upon the bound Man
    led to stand directly before him.

Jesus,
    remember me,
    when you come into your Kingdom.

Annas,
    the father-in-law
    of the current High Priest, Caiaphas,
        studies this Jesus intently.
He smirks and walks around the Prisoner.

Annas has wanted
    to get close to Jesus for some time now.
And since the events of Sunday
    and Jesus' attack on the Temple markets,
        Annas was determined
            to capture this Jesus.
Tonight He is here.

Jesus,
    remember me,
    when you come into your Kingdom.

The powers of darkness
    are gathering
        around the walls of the room,
        around this house
    and, in particular,
        around the courtyard.

Annas studies
    the features of this Jesus.
He notices no marks of renown
    or any hints of greatness.
This would-be Messiah looks so ordinary,
    so average, Annas thinks.

What did we have to fear
    from this simple misguided village rabbi?
Why all this commotion
    and this rush?
How could the masses have been
    so deceived, so duped
        by a small-minded Man
        with grandiose ambitions?
How could the Sanhedrin be
    so concerned, so frightened
        by such an ordinary Man?
He is nothing more than a fake and a fraud.

He stands silent before Annas...
    and He is bound.
He seems so insignificant.
    Why all this concern?
    Why the rush to arrest?

Jesus,
    remember me,
    when you come into your Kingdom.

Annas wants this matter
    resolved here this night.
Images of the Temple courtyard in shambles
    enters his mind and memory.
Tables of money changers strewn all about,
    animals running every which way
    and the people fleeing from the Temple.
Annas calculated the thousands of shekels lost,
    and his blood begins to boil.

Who was this Man
   who alone could shut down
     the business of the Temple?
Certainly He was and is dangerous.
   He was and is a rebel, not a rabbi,
   a criminal and not a healer.
The people are simple sheep
   who blindly follow anyone
     who performs feats of magic
     and fills their bellies with bread.

The people must be protected,
   the worship of Yahweh must be kept pure,
   the Temple must be preserved,
   and the nation safeguarded.
This Man must be stopped!
We must put an end to His ministry
   and the silencing of His followers.
The sheep will then follow
   the true shepherds of Israel:
     Annas, Caiaphas, and the Sanhedrin!

Jesus,
   remember me,
   when you come into your Kingdom.

This matter of Jesus must be handled…
   delicately but quickly.
Cooperation will be needed from three persons:
   Pilate, Herod and Caiaphas.
     A strange grouping indeed,

an unholy alliance,
    a distorted trinity.
Pilate desired order,
Herod loyalty,
and Caiaphas obedience.

Jesus was a major disruption
    in the very workings of the
        Empire, Kingdom and Temple.

Jesus and His ministry
    required an obedience and a loyalty
    that was creating a new order.

Pilate had no taste for religion.
    A Messiah meant nothing to him.
But a Jew called a king in the streets?
    Pilate takes notice – this cannot stand!
To Annas, he orders:
    "Take care of this matter or I will!"

Herod did not mind having Annas and Caiaphas
    squirm under the gaze of Pilate.
Oh, yes, these men met,
    they argued,
    they compromised,
    they agreed.
Jesus must be dealt with!

"It is better for one man to die
    than for the entire nation to perish!"

Herod was hoping
   that Pilate would make a mistake.
Pilate would be delighted
   if Caiaphas and his Sanhedrin blundered.
He also pondered how Jesus could be used
   as a pawn to make Herod and Pilate
   look like fools before the people.

The stakes are high
   and each is willing to gamble
   on the ultimate prize: Power!

The Man stands before Annas
   who craves and desires power.
Pilate had robbed him of it
   when he stripped him of the High Priesthood
   and gave the title instead to Caiaphas,
   his son-in-law.

Annas remained powerful
   but he secretly seethed
   at his loss of status and prestige.
He held Pilate liable and he wanted revenge.

Jesus,
   remember me,
   when you come into your Kingdom.

Annas questions.
   Jesus remains silent.
Annas demands.
   Jesus remains silent.

Annas rants and raves.
   Jesus remains silent.

A guard roughs Jesus up
   because His silence is seen
   as disrespect to Annas.
"Lead Him to Caiaphas.
   Let him deal with this Man."
Having encountered Jesus,
   Annas cannot fully understand all the panic.

This Jesus is no threat.
   What were they so nervous about?
Without His followers and magic
   this Man is no Messiah.
Just a poor fool who believed His own press
   and claim to fame.

Jesus,
   remember me,
   when you come into your Kingdom.

Under the cover of night
   evil seizes the hour.
And in the house of Caiaphas,
   under the cloak of legality,
   a makeshift court assembles.

The stage is set,
   the verdict obtained,
   the players assemble

and – unknown to them –
they do the will of the Father.

As if he were in control,
    Caiaphas opens this court of dishonor
    and calls forth witnesses
    to fabricate the truth.

Jesus,
    the very essence of Truth,
    stands before them,
    a silent observer to His own demise.

He raises no protest,
    utters no defense.
All the while
    the henchmen of deceit
    weave their lies.

Meanwhile in the courtyard
    within sight and earshot of the trial
    sits a Galilean fisherman by trade…
        no Apostle tonight.

Warmed by the fire
    on this cold bleak night
    a number of people
    approach this big man
    to inquire about his plight.

The fisherman,
    normally the picture of cool,

loses his temper,
and starts to scream and shout.

A rooster crows
   a glance is given.
Jesus has heard the denials.
   Peter is exposed.

Jesus,
   remember me,
   when you come into your Kingdom.

Peter – soon to be the Rock – is crushed
   as he remembers the words of Jesus
   just hours before.
Crestfallen and despondent
   he flees the courtyard and
   a second time on this strange night,
   he leaves his Master alone
   to face His judge and jury –
   not his peers but his accusers and henchmen.

The Prince of Peace
   is in the clutches of the prince of darkness.

Meanwhile,
   the halls of Heaven have fallen silent
   as the betrayal and the denial reverberate
   throughout the vaulted Kingdom of Light.
Angels lower their heads.
   Grief is experienced in the celestial domain.

The Cherubim are silent.
No hosannas echo before the throne.
The face of the Father grows grey.
The very Light of the Universe grows dim.
Heaven is growing cold
as the host of Heaven look down
and gaze in utter sorrow
upon the scene as it unfolds.

Jesus,
remember me,
when you come into your Kingdom.

The Kingdom of Praise is voiceless.
The Kingdom of Light goes dark.
The Kingdom of Truth is silenced.
Truth is held prisoner
in the grasp of the deceiver.

Beyond the path of Light,
through the gaze of good,
our sight
descends to the realm of darkness
to the abode of evil
to the kingdom of Lucifer.

There is within this realm
pandemonium and savage joy
for He who is called the Son
is within Satan's grasp.

This realm can sniff the blood,
    an elixir of grace perverted
    and of love turned rancid.
Demons and deposed angels
    dance and laugh;
    they chant songs of blasphemy;
    they mock the Throne of God.

In this realm of darkness
    hate and terror wed.
For on this unholy night,
    sin and death are breaking free
      to pursue the final conquest,
      to destroy love,
      vanquish grace,
      and subjugate creation.

Myriads of demons
    are ready for the final assault.
The glee and cacophony of chaos
    delights the master of this dark world.

The master,
    once a great angel of Light,
    is now an image of decrepit corruption,
    of celestial beauty decayed.
A being deformed
    hears an Apostle deny his Lord
    and clasps his hands in devious delight.
One denial is great;
    a second, simply superb;

but a third is certainly profound.
Peter, we await your arrival
　　into this realm of sin and guilt and shame.
You will find a home here!

Welcome!
A place at my right hand awaits you
　　for we do reward all those
　　who attack God and disown His Son!

Jesus,
　　remember me,
　　when you come into your Kingdom.

The forces of the realm of darkness
　　mount an assault.
One of the twelve betrays!
　　Another denies!
　　　　And all the rest flee!
How simple it is
　　to master this human race!

Ah! But grace is yet
　　to make its presence felt –
On this night, though, there is a chill
　　for the blanket of grace
　　is yet to cover the children of Adam and Eve
　　　　who are cold
　　　　because sin
　　　　has captured the human heart.

Do we ever stop to consider the coldness of sin,
    for sin possesses not the warmth of love
    but only emptiness and shame?

Christ, the essence of love,
    is surrounded now by the coldness of sin
    and the realm of darkness
    where an arctic air blows.
In the eyes of Satan there is delight
    for in his grasp
    is the mystery
    soon to be dissolved into a memory.
Ah! Victory so sweet,
    oh, battle so easily won.

But wait!
    What do I see?
Creeping along the avenues of this city
    a fisherman crouches beside a cold stone wall.
Is that weeping that I see and hear?

Meanwhile, an anguished cry
    and heartfelt scream
        is heard within the halls of Hell
    for Satan is about to lose his hold
        over that poor fisherman,
    the one who would be a leader,
        the one whom Satan thought he had found
        so easy to control and mold.
With his tears of sorrow and repentance,
    this Apostle slips
        through the fingertips of Satan.

Contrition fouls Satan's plans.
   A heart touched by this Son of God
      he cannot possess.
Peter's cries of sorrow infuriate Lucifer.
The King of Hell has been made a fool;
   the demons around the great deceiver crouch,
      for rage is about to be released.

Satan is angry
   and Hell shakes!

Jesus,
   remember me,
   when you come into your Kingdom.

Satan screams and covers his head
   so that he cannot hear or see
   the scene as it unfolds.
A mere human cries
   and a God forgives denial.
Love momentarily holds the time of evil at bay.

Satan scoffs at this display of human emotion
   and the weakness of a God
   who demonstrates such mercy.
Satan despises this Deity
   who showers His creatures
   with such compassion.
The face of evil becomes twisted and deformed.
The Evil One cares not
   for the weakness of this God,
   this God who is his sworn enemy.

33

"Enough!
  I have lost the fisherman for now," he says.
Glee emanates from the face of Lucifer
    as he turns his attention to the house of Annas
    and the trial of that "holy" Man.

"The Son is the prize!
  I'll attend to this weeping fisherman
      another time."

Jesus,
  remember me,
  when you come into your Kingdom.

"There is no Kingdom of God," Satan rants.
  "Only the domain of Hell."

Daylight begins timidly to appear,
  shamed to give light to the travesty
      that Satan weaves
      with the threads of evil, sin and hate.

The light floods into the courtroom,
  declaring the trial to be adjourned.
The witnesses and judge are all fatigued.
The prisoner is escorted to a cell.

Satan laughs!
  Sin and evil dance!
      God is going to die!

The cell that holds Divinity
  is dark and damp and cold.

On this night
  humanity has made God a prisoner.
And laughter is heard from the bowels of Hell.

  The prisoner – alone –
    is tired,
      in fact fatigued.
He has not slept for nights
  prior to the unfolding of the darkness
    that now covers the earth.
It is not the darkness of night
  but the blackness of sin
  and the triumph of evil.

Heaven shudders,
  humanity sleeps
  and Hell delights!

The prisoner stands,
  weary arms outstretched,
  and begins to pray.
In the time between night and morning's first light,
  the Son of God utters His prayer:
"Abba, Father,
  Your will be done."
He says it over and over again.
  It is a cry.
  It is an appeal.
  It is an act of submission!

"Abba, Father,
  Your will be done."

Again and again.
His bruised and cracked lips
    utter the phrase over and over again.

The prayer begins its work
    of healing the wounded heart.
The eyes, once vacant,
    are now inflamed with passion.
Shoulders, once hunched,
    are now straightened with determination.

Again the prayer is uttered:

"Abba, Father,
    Your will be done."

A jailer listens at the door.
The prayer resonates and touches something
    in the jailer's gruff exterior.
He moves closer to the cell door.
In the usually cold, damp dungeon
    the jailer experiences a warmth
    as he draws near the cell.

He glances at the praying figure.
There is a serenity and unusual calm
    for a Man at the center
    of a political and religious storm.
From the otherwise darkened area
    a glow and strange light
    emanates from the cell.

The jailer notes
   that there is no source of natural light,
   nor a flame made by a vessel filled with oil.
None of these were there
   and yet the light prevails.

The glow of the light,
   the strange warmth,
   and the ceaseless prayer
   have deeply puzzled him.

The jailer become a prisoner for the moment.
   He stares around him.
   He sees the Man,
   and he utters his own prayer:
"Yahweh,
   watch over this strange and fearless Man."

This Man had unnerved Annas
   who himself could make a Roman tremble.

The trial did not go well.
   The carpenter was no fool.
Neither Annas nor Caiaphas
      nor the forces of Rome
   could frighten this rabbi
   and would-be Messiah.
They slapped and mocked Him
   who just days earlier rode into this city
   declared by the people to be its king.
   And now He is the city's most wanted.

In spite of such treatment
  He remained a person in control and dignified.
Meanwhile, the members of the Sanhedrin
  who were present
  seem confused and erratic,
  more like a mob than a religious group.

The rabbi stood straight and composed
  with an air of integrity,
  purpose
  and determination.
His will, touched by the Divine, was strong
  and would not yield.
They could not bend Him
  to their purpose or intent.

Jesus,
  remember me,
  when you come into your Kingdom.

The kingdoms of this world, led by Satan,
  are prepared to do battle
  with the Kingdom of God.
The forces are arrayed;
  the army of evil is poised to strike
  the Word of God.
They prefer the deafening sounds of silence
  to the Word of God
  speaking, revealing, loving and healing.

As the morning sun rises slowly in the East,
  two figures glance at one another –

the prisoner and His jailer.
A final prayer is uttered;
   the carpenter is ready.
Sorrowfully, the jailer opens the door
   knowing that he must lead this Man
   to face His judge and His destiny.

Little does the jailer know
   that the prisoner's destiny
   is the jailer's future.

Gracious Lord,
   This is now the turning point
      of Salvation History.
As these hours unfold,
   God will be silent
   but God's promise will be fulfilled this day.

Jesus,
   remember me,
   when you come into your Kingdom.

Morning light replaces the glow
   of a Man anointed by prayer and acceptance.
The jailer apologizes
   as he ties His hands behind His back…
   hands that so often
   simply touched and healed so many
   cannot reach out today
   and heal a broken world.
And still, as morning breaks,
   though He may not touch physically

with hands thus bound,
He will surely, by day's end,
heal, forgive and give New Life.

The prisoner, bound, looks to be at peace
as He begins His ascent up the stairs
that will lead to a new day of grace and hope.
Within His heart He prays,
"Father, Your will be done!"

Jesus,
remember me,
when you come into your Kingdom.

Friday Morning

As the sun begins its rise
　　in this city of ancient faith and worship,
　　a lone man is seen plodding along
　　　　– in a daze and in confusion –
　　along the narrow streets.
He is a man beset by demons.

He runs,
　　then stops,
　　　　then races again and stops.

Judas, where are you running from?
　　Judas, where are you running to?
Judas, it is not too late.
　　Return to Him.
　　　　The fisherman did!
Judas, there is no place to hide.
　　Run back to Him.
　　　　He will forgive you.

The face is tortured in its grief;
　　the soul is hounded by its guilt.
The mind is ablaze with shame;

the heart is empty
    with the worthless glitter of silver.

Judas, did you not hear the Master?
    "Love your enemies,
        bless those who harm you."
Judas, stop running.
    Remember, believe, repent!

Judas feels the heaviness of the silver.

What once was delightful
    has now become an awful burden.
        He can hardly carry the weight.
The silver is now too much
    of a burden for him to bear.
He casts it down to the ground.
He stares at the pouch
    recalling the face of Jesus in the garden.
He shakes his head
    as if to dispel the image.
        But he cannot.

Jesus,
    How could I betray you with a kiss?

A coldness envelops him
    but it is not the chill of the air
        that makes him shiver.
It was the look of Jesus
    just a few hours ago in the Garden.
Judas recalls the day he and Jesus met.

It was nearly three years ago
    when word began to spread
        of a rabbi who teaches and heals.

Curiosity had gripped Judas then.
He journeyed to Cana to see the man
    whom so many were seeking
        to find,
        to see,
        to touch,
        to hear.

At a wedding feast he sees the Man.
He was so ordinary and calm,
    so relaxed among family and friends.
In such a company
    the ordinary turns extraordinary.
Water becomes wine,
    the average turns spectacular
        touched by the supernatural.

The Man invites: "Come, follow Me!"
    Judas – enthralled – responds:
        "Yes, I will!"
And so he leaves behind what little he has
    and walks with this Man
    to seek the dream:
        the Kingdom of God.
For Jesus, it is a Kingdom not of this world.
    Judas, however, seeks one
        in the here and now.

Visions clash,
  and yet he follows.
He is entrusted with the company's money –
  This is where his hopes and treasures lie.
If only Jesus would just change His style.

The Master knows, but still holds hope
  that Judas will see the light.
Judas has seen
  the lame walk,
  the blind see,
  the hungry fed,
  the dead restored.
But the money belt entices with a hidden touch.
  It calls and he grasps the pouch tight.

Jesus offers you sight
  but you will not see;
Jesus grants you grace
  but you struggle with sin.
Jesus invites you to truth
  that will set you free,
    but the coins in your pouch
      make you struggle and fall.

The years pass – three in all.
  You are still unconvinced of Jesus' call.
The Apostles are weary of you;
  no friend do they consider you,
    no intimate companion.

Of Him – the Christ – you are not convinced.
   A fool, you think. He cannot be the One.

But remorse,
   shame,
   guilt,
   and fear
      cloud your heart
         and you dance instead
         with the Demon.

Satan lost Peter
   but you he holds firm.
Your heart is in agony
   and Satan will not let go.

Something grasps and captures you.
   Is it repentance?
Satan howls and screams,
   for the man
      who betrayed and kissed the Lord
      is about to undo what he has done.
He races to the Temple
   with the silver in tow
      to ransom back
      what was bought with malice.

Satan is in a panic
   for he is about to lose Judas.

To the Temple Judas flies;
   he enters the chambers of the priests.

"I've changed my mind;
   here is the silver.
      Let Jesus go,
          and let it all be undone."

They gaze, stunned at this feeble man
   and at such a ridiculous suggestion.
They laugh.
   "See to it yourself!
       What is done is done!"

The noose gnaws tighter
   and Satan snags Judas for one last fall.
To the floor,
   the silver tossed tumbles in disarray.
Judas is freed and races up a lonely hill.

The Prince of Darkness has clouded his mind –
   "What you have done, no one can forgive.
       It is better had you never been born."

And so to a hill
   in a frenzy he flees.
"What have I done?
   Why have I done this?
Can anyone hear me?
   Can anyone help?"

But there is only silence!

"Judas, all is lost –
   you are alone.

There is no one to forgive you,
　　for the One who could do so
　　is bound and on His way to His own hill."
Judas despairs.

Satan, in glee,
　　propels the traitor to a decaying tree.

　　"Go ahead! Do it!
　　　　There is no other way.
　　End it!
　　　　Your life is useless anyway."

So, with halter in hand, a noose he ties.
　　His heart is heavy.

Within just moments
　　the branch,
　　the noose,
　　the neck snaps.
The breath retreats,
　　the eyes close,
　　a heart stops beating.
The wind picks up,
　　the body sways,
　　the limb snaps,
　　the traitor falls.

Judas is dead upon a hill facing Calvary
　　where Life will soon face death
　　　　surrounded by love and tears.
On *this* hill, no one grieves.

Satan dances,
    heaven moans.
The clouds darken
    but the day has just begun.

When the limb snapped,
    the Master – bound –
    felt in His heart
        the beating heart of a lost sheep.
The Shepherd always feels such a loss.
The Christ – betrayed –
    mourns the loss of the one who,
        through the centuries,
    will always bear the name of "Traitor."

Jesus,
    remember me,
    when you come into your Kingdom.

"Father, Your will be done.
    I am ready for the tree that awaits."

But not before Pilate, Caiaphas and history
    have spun their web of intrigue.

Seated now upon a seat of judgment,
    Caiaphas reads the sentence –
        "Blasphemy. The penalty is death!"

To the Roman now
    he must present this Man,
    this charge,

this final victory
      over the rabbi
            who has sore distressed
            the House of Israel.
Let this matter finally be put to rest.

Jesus,
      remember me,
      when you come into your Kingdom.

Roaming the streets,
      forlorn and deeply distressed,
            Cephas
      – called by Jesus to be the rock –
            still weeps.
Tears streaming down his face
      he enters the Cenacle.
Silence greets him
      although the room is filled
            with ten other frightened men.
Now the eleven
      – assembled in fear and disbelief –
            look towards Peter
            for a sign of courage
            or a message of hope.

He weeps uncontrollably
      and – unashamed –
            admits his denials
            and seeks their comfort.

All is lost, the mission is dead
   their rabbi and leader gone –
  at this moment on trial.
The group is alone
   for the Shepherd is gone.

The table is still set
   bearing the plate and the cup
    and they all recall –
      "Do this in memory of Me!"

When Jesus needed them,
   they all ran.
When Jesus was arrested,
   He stood there alone.
When Jesus was dragged
   before the leaders of the people
    no one was present
    to offer His defense.

The youngest stands
   and confronts the silence and the group.
"We can't just stay here and hide
   while our Master and Lord
    suffers the indignation of arrest
    and the mockery of a trial.

"Our Master spoke of love and peace;
   Our world and its leaders
   have reacted with violence and hate.

"Our Lord fed thousands;
   last night we celebrated with Him
     the Passover,
  which may well be His
    and our last supper.
Jesus raised the dead to life,
  and now His own life is in peril.
Yet here we sit and hide.
  But what could we possibly do
    to help Him now?
  We could risk our lives
    and accomplish nothing.
He has too many followers.
  He is too well known.
Those in authority
  will not impose the death penalty,
  for there will be rioting in the streets."

Another speaks and voices harshly
  that all of us are fools.
"If we, His chosen few, have fled and now hide,
  frightened for our lives,
   do we truly believe that others will rise
   and demand that He be set free?

"Under cover of night they arrested Him,
  and now before the city wakes,
  His fate will be sealed.

"He spoke often in the last few weeks
  of His impending arrest and death.

The cross, He says, awaits
    and we must be willing to carry our own.
But He will first pave the way.

"Last night He predicted – rightly –
    that one of us would betray Him
        and another would deny Him.
This morning both have come true."

Jesus,
    remember me,
    when you come into your Kingdom.

"Enough talk," the beloved disciple bellows.
    "I will not hide
        but will stand
        with my Master and my Lord."

He flees the room
    and runs to where his Lord stands trial.
The others, held by fear and shame,
    bolt the door and keep a vigil
        – a vigil for death –
    for this Passover week
    the Angel of Death
        will not pass over
        this room or city.

The quiet streets this morning
    echo with the sound of one Apostle
        racing through this city
        of faith and history.

He must find his Lord and Master
and stand by Him.
He should not be left to stand alone.

"Whatever His fate
and whatever the risk
I will share because I love Him
and will not abandon Him."

He goes weaving through the streets –
first to the house of Annas....
But a servant advises him to go to the Temple
and to the Sanhedrin.
"There you will find Him whom you seek."

So to the Temple he now runs
as the morning rays of light
fall upon his path.
The courts are now filling with pilgrims
but the environment is heavy
– not with prayers and sacrifice –
but with frenzy over the news and commotion.
"The rabbi from Nazareth,
the carpenter who arrived last Sunday
– hailed as a king –
is now arrested and stands before our leaders."

So the arrest is known;
it will not go uncontested.
His followers will not stand for this travesty.

The people do not fear the Man
   but see Him as their hope and Savior.

Jesus,
   remember me,
   when you come into your Kingdom.

The Apostle listens attentively
   to gather information
   about his Lord and Master's whereabouts.
The crowd is streaming towards the fort
      – Antonia by name –
   and in the air he hears the news:
The Sanhedrin has found the carpenter guilty;
   the charge is blasphemy!

Pilate must now review the case
   and pass the sentence.
If he agrees with the verdict
   he will impose the penalty –
      Death by Crucifixion!

John stood anchored in disbelief.
How could they find Him guilty,
   this man of love and peace?
Surely, Pilate will see through this ruse
   and lift the veil of jealousy
   that has prompted the priests
   to behave like a mob of thugs.

The crowd – now a mob –
   converges on the courtyard.

The din of many voices rises
    as this sea of people stand
        anxious and excited
    before the Roman lord
        seated on his throne of judgment.

Then a hush falls over the scene.
All eyes travel upward
    to that portico and seat.
Then, there is an audible gasp
    as the Man enters the scene
        and faces His judge.

The Man looks pitiful and forlorn.
His tunic is soiled
    with mud and dirt and spittle.
His face is bruised
    from the slaps and punches
        administered by the guards
        in need of a victim and a jest.

John would give anything
    to stand beside his Lord
        and let Him know He is not alone.
The crowd – thick and unruly –
    presses forward.
Pilate – with a wave of his hand –
    demands silence.

"I have heard the charges
    leveled by your leaders."

The governor speaks,
   the crowd listens intently.
"And I find the charges unfounded.
   I find no fault in this Man.
      I will release Him."

John can scarcely believe his ears.
Pilate – the Roman and unbeliever –
   will set Jesus free.
What a stroke of pure luck!
But more than just luck:
   Yahweh's grace
   has touched the heart of a Gentile.

The halls of Hell, though,
   will not hear of such foolish talk,
      such nonsense.
   This Man must not be set free.
He must be forced
   to carry the wood,
   embrace the beam
   and feel the nails.

Evil this day has many faces.
Within this mob Satan unleashes
   a desire for blood
   a hunger for death,
   a passion for violence,
   a taste for brutality.

The mob is excited.

The sight of the Man stirs a primitive instinct:
    they want His blood;
    they demand His life.

"I find no guilt in this Man."

The crowd surges forward
    not in mercy but in degrees of rage.

"What has this Man done
    that I should take His life?"
Pilate knows that the Man is innocent.
    He is wavering.
    He is confused.
    He is becoming frightened.

The mob is uneasy,
    moving closer to the place
        where the Man stands
        and the governor sits.
Pilate – usually in control –
    begins to perspire.
The sweat forms on his brow,
    beads appear and roll down his face.
With a cloth by his side
    he dabs at his face.
His hands begin to shake.
He thinks, "Why does this Man,
    a Prisoner, rattle me so?"

The crowd is unruly now
    and growing impatient.

Pilate suddenly recalls
a custom from the past.
Perhaps this will soothe the crowd
and allow the Man to be set free.
The Man meant nothing to Pilate,
but having control was key.
Pilate had to be in charge;
he will not be swayed
by a mob or by its priests.
These Jews belong to Rome
and not I to them.

This rabble and their insignificant nation
with their unseen God
is testing Pilate's patience.
He will force the mob to do his will
and not that of Caiaphas.
The High Priest stands mute,
his cronies surrounding him.
Pilate's eyes and his meet;
distrust darts
from one glance to the other.

Meanwhile,
the Lord of Hell
unleashes legions of demons
to infiltrate the mob.
Satan will take control for Pilate
and Caiaphas will do his will.
These puny mortals think they matter.

How very foolish they are.
And yet this God loves them.
Who is the bigger fool?
He, the Creator,
   or these men and women
   who had once declared Jesus to be a king
   and now desire His blood?

The Man – bloodied and alone –
   stands apart,
      a figure of lost hope
      and an image of despair,
   flanked by Pilate and the surging mob.

Alone, perhaps, but not frightened.
It is Pilate who trembles
   before a mob bent and driven
   by the smell and taste of blood.

Meanwhile, legions of demons stand by the gate
   waiting for the command to march.
They have watched the mob,
   their appetite whetted.
They spy the prey.
   They are hungry.
And here there are
   souls aplenty,
   a governor confused,
   priests intent,
   and a Man who is beaten.

"What need have we of witnesses?"
The plan is well conceived:
 Truth will die upon a tree.

Pilate –
 a man accustomed to power and command –
 barks orders.
His wishes are obeyed,
 his frown and displeasure to be avoided.

A man of flesh and blood,
 who craved comfort,
 whose hands were smooth and clean,
 whose clothing was expensive,
 covering a body often pampered.
How often had he raised a perfumed hand
   to his nose
 to conceal the stench of these foreigners
 and this barbaric land.

To please Caesar,
 Pilate had obeyed
 and journeyed to this land
 of Jews and zealots.
How he preferred the avenues of Rome
 to the dusty roads of Palestine.
His assignment to govern a backward people
 was just a stepping-stone
 on his return to Rome
 where he believed he truly belonged.

But today this stepping-stone
    has become very slippery.
A wandering Jewish rabbi might well cause
    his dreams and ambitions to disappear.
Anger welled up within him
    as he eyed the Man
    who could become his undoing.

As he stood and stared at the Man,
    bound and beaten,
he realized that the mob before him
    was intent on bending his will
        and doing their bidding.

The sun – already at midpoint –
    blazed upon the crowd,
    inflaming their temper
    and adding fire to their frenzied mood.

Jesus,
    remember me,
    when you come into your Kingdom.

Pilate was hesitating
    and with each misstep the mob
        sensed weakness
        and became emboldened.
They surged forward.
    The mob would not be silenced.
It will be heard,
    its presence felt,
    its ugly mood apparent.

Satan saw an opening
    for his final assault.
The Man was doomed,
    the Creator's plans will be foiled.
Lucifer smelled victory.
    It was a scent he relished.
He gave the order to the demons
    waiting for his command.
With glee he voiced the order:
    Infiltrate the mob;
    be sure of the outcome.
    The Man must die!

With a demonic gesture of his hand,
    wave after wave of demons
    rushed through a hole
    in the cave of Hell
    and were ushered down a darkened hall
    towards an opening
    that led to the created world.
Before the demons lay a remarkable sight:
    creation in all its glory:
    stars and planets,
    galaxies and shooting stars and supernovas.
For a moment,
    legions of devils halt
    as the magnificence of the universe
        envelops them.
For just a brief period of time
    these custodians of evil were struck with awe

as the canopy of the world lighted their way
to the small blue planet
that humanity calls home.

The mob was totally unaware
of the cosmic proportions
now unfolding before them
and possessing them all.

Pilate, too, was preoccupied
with his own thoughts.
He failed to perceive the subtle shift
in the mood, tempo and pace of the crowd.
He assumed he was in charge,
but the myriads of demons
were in a disharmony of delight
feeding the minds of this now captured race.

A whispering demon has the ear of the governor.
(He thinks himself quite intelligent
because of the plan that he has conceived.)
Facing the crowd,
Pilate raises his arms and calls for silence.
"You have a custom during this time of Passover
which Rome wishes to honor."

As he speaks, a prison door below
in the Fort Antonia swings open.
From the darkness
Barabbas emerges into the afternoon light:
a zealot,
a murderer,

a prisoner,
and now a pawn.

On one side, Jesus the rabbi:
   bloody, bruised,
   eyes vacant and swollen,
   clothing torn and dirty,
   head crowned with thorns,
   body rent with scourges and revealing gaps,
   tears in the flesh,
   hands tied,
   and head bowed.

On the other side, the criminal, Barabbas:
   burly and arrogant,
   standing tall and erect,
   eyes surveying the crowd,
   wondering why this show
   and not the path with a cross.
Early this morning he had been waiting
   for the guards to lead him out to Calvary.

The crossbeam lay unattended
   but visible enough for Barabbas to see
   and to realize his fate was sealed.
He would die today upon a hill
   and suffer horror before his last breath.
This man of steel and guts
   shivered at the thought.
But as the door opened
   he was paraded before the seat of judgment.

Already condemned,
  why the need
  to stand before the governor and this mob?

Then in the morning sunlight
  he sees the Man
  covered in blood,
  head bowed,
    and Barabbas is stunned and stares.

He realizes they have been asked
  to make a choice:
Barabbas the terrorist
  or Jesus the rabbi.
He has no chance;
  the sympathy will be
  with that pathetic-looking do-gooder.
What a rout!
  This Pilate is no fool.

Everyone in the mob,
  this crowd of Jews,
  his fellow countrymen
  are calling him by name....
  "We want Barabbas!"

Pilate is caught off guard;
  Barabbas is shocked.
He thought it was nothing more
  than a cruel Roman joke.
But there was no mistake!

Barabbas could distinctly hear the crowd repeat
    again and again:
        "We want Barabbas,
            We want Barabbas!"
Something clearly was going on here
    that Pilate and Barabbas
        could not fully comprehend.
Pilate glares at Barabbas
    who, in turn, gives the governor
        a sinister sneer.
The governor has lost control.
    The mob screams louder and louder.
Pilate raises his hands for silence.
    It takes a while for his wish to be obeyed.
When the crowd was dutifully obedient,
    Pilate would send them into a rage,
        a blood lust.

Pointing to the blood-stained Man
    whose head was still bowed, he asked:
    "What am I to do with Jesus, your King?"

Satan jumps with joy.
Filled with glee, his face is transformed
    by an evil and cruel smile,
        his features turn from ugly to decay.

The life of the Son is his;
    the Father has lost.
His own creation has turned against Him
    once again and rebelled.

The Son came to love and save this human race.
Though divinely touched, the people respond
    by rejecting the Father's gift.
The Son came to embrace and save,
    but these children of Adam and Eve
    are so easy to deceive.

The hands of evil have worked the crowd
    and massaged their minds to do his will.
His voice whispers into willing ears;
    his commands find easy partners
      for his devious plans.

Again, Pilate demands…
    indeed nearly pleads:
      "What am I to do with this Man?"

The air is scented with a foul smell;
    the crowd screams in barbaric tones:
      "Crucify Him! Take Him to the cross!"
Golgotha beckons and calls for Him.
    "Away with Him!"
The air hangs heavy with a putrid aroma –
    hate mixed with blood and it is lethal.

The cacophony of yells,
    screams
    and shouts
    are in no way exhausted.
Satan, as a master conductor,
    raises his hands

and the choir once more
chants their eulogy for the Son:
    "Crucify Him! Crucify Him!"

Satan is about to destroy the Master's plan
    and will use His own creation
        to foul and distort Salvation.
According to his design
    he will destroy the bond of love
        the Creator so patiently weaves.
The threads now unravel
    and the beautiful rope
        hung down from Heaven in order to save
        snaps and breaks.

Pilate – disgusted now –
    and out of options
    summons a servant
    who enters the eternal fray
    carrying a bowl of water
    and a crisp white towel.
He approaches the governor
    before the judgment seat.
Frustrated, Pilate calls for silence
    and will use a gesture
    to finally close the case.

Defeated, he addresses the crowd
    with unsure voice.
        "I find no fault in this Man."

Then he dramatically washes his hands and states,
  "I wash my hands of the blood of this
  innocent Man.
    See to it yourselves!"

Water flows over his hands,
  but it is not soothing.
  In fact, it fairly stings his flesh.
He grabs the towel
  and frantically attempts to wipe them
  dry and clean.

What a perversion!
The night before,
  the Man had taken water and a towel
  and with love and a humble heart
  He knelt and washed the feet of the men
  He tenderly loved and loves –
  the same men who
    fled from Him,
    denied Him,
    and betrayed Him.
He had given them a new command:
  "Love one another as I love you."

The servant missteps.
  The bowl falls and shatters before the crowd.
    The pottery breaks,
    the water spills,
    the grand gesture
    is now lost in the laughter of the mob.

Barabbas glares at Pilate
    and raises his hands still tied.
The call to release him is given to a centurion
    who, at first protests,
        but is forced to obey,
            helpless before the impotent rage
            of Pontius Pilate
            and his vanishing authority.

With a flash of steel,
    a raised sword snaps the bonds
    that held his hands.
He is free and is pushed down the stairs
    to stand with the crowd
    that had made him their friend.
He is free as he descends and turns once more
    to look at the Man
    who will carry *his* cross to Calvary.

As he looks up at Him,
    the bowed head lifts
    and his eyes gaze at the zealot.
The bloodied rabbi is ready
    to walk the path to Calvary.
And Barabbas, a man with bloodied hands,
    is made clean and freed
    by this carpenter and teacher.
Pushed into the crowd,
    Barabbas gets lost.
But the eyes of the rabbi
    have penetrated his soul.

70

He can't forget the look.
He is momentarily free,
  but will forever be haunted
    by those eyes,
    that glance,
    that bloody form.
The rabbi is now called a criminal
  because he had delusions of being a king.
The Man now leads a dismal procession
  of soldiers, guards and onlookers.
He bears on His shoulders a crossbeam
  as He slowly moves along the path
  that leads to the place they call the Skull.

How odd…,
  for the crossbeam should have been his
  but now they are hoisting it upon the back
  of a Man some call a prophet and a healer.

Barabbas wades through the crowd
  receiving congratulatory slaps on his back.
A murderer becomes a hero
  and a compassionate, loving Man
  is dragged down the road towards hell.

Meanwhile
  in the chambers of the governor's residence,
  a man robed in the purple of power
  sits forlorn,
    his face depicting defeat
    as he scowls at the assembled group.

How did this case go so wrong?
Why is a killer set free
    and a man of God about to die?

Pilate signs the decree of execution
    tossing it to the centurion
    charged with its implementation.
It is a gruesome task,
    one that he carries out without emotion,
    absent of any care
    except for the Roman devotion to time
    and the perfection of form and style.

The Path of Sorrow

The chilling procession of death
   begins its serpentine march,
    surrounded by unseen gleeful demons
     and angels with bowed heads,
    shedding tears
     for this pitiful and pathetic Man –
The Son this day
    has become the rejected of His race
    and of the people He was sent to save.

This procession of death begins its sorrowful path
   through the narrow streets
     of this ancient and sacred city
     now soiled by this unholy sight.

This path will become well known
   throughout the ages.
But today this comedy of evil
   is an annoyance for the people
   rushing to and fro…
    unaware that they are silent witnesses
     to a moment in history

when God chose to cast the shadow
    of the cross
to save this rebellious humanity.

It is nearly the noon hour
    and the streets of this city of Jerusalem
    are bustling with many people.
And in the air there is the scent of excitement
    for this is the week of Passover celebration.

The Temple is teeming with the faithful,
    the surrounding courtyards
    are filled to near capacity.

Houses are being prepared for the evening meal
    for this holy night
    and, indeed, the whole week of celebration,
    recalls the power of Yahweh
    to save His people.
As they remember God saving them in the past
    they miss the glory of God
        reaching out to save all of us
        from the grasp of Satan.

On this typical and very ordinary afternoon,
    vendors in the street are selling their goods
    and bargaining for the best price!

Children are seen racing to and fro,
    playing and laughing
        all over this celebrating city

unaware that in one corner of it
an event has taken place.
For on a very ordinary day
a man had taken a bowl of water
and washed his hands.
The act,
though a simple gesture,
has this day cosmic implications.

The Man now carries the wood.
He hardly looks like a man –
eyes swollen,
face battered and bruised,
body beaten and still bleeding.

Behold the Man!
His lips are cracked,
his face is covered
in blood,
dirt,
spit
and sweat.
His head is covered in a gruesome crown of thorns,
His hair is matted with drying blood.
He is an awful sight to behold,
but still there is a dignity and grace
that not only defies
but now defines the moment.

How often do we wash our hands of Christ?

Jesus,
   remember me,
   when you come into your Kingdom.

Behold the wood of the Cross!
This way of sorrows beckons us
   to watch this journey to the Hill.

Recall how the rabbi said,
   "Come to Me all of you who are burdened
      and I will give you rest"?

The crossbeam weighs nearly a hundred pounds,
   the gentle rabbi struggles and weaves –
He is exhausted and tired;
   each step is pure torture.

Who will aid the Man to carry this weight,
   this burden of the world,
   on such fragile but willing shoulders?

Yahweh whispers to the gawking crowd,
   "What burdens do you carry?
      What weighs you down?
   What sin?
      What hurt?
   What pain?
      What loss?
My Son carries all of these and more besides."

Imagine for a moment
   the carpenter who cut the wood

that the rabbi would carry,
the cross the soldiers
would lay upon His shoulders.

The weight is just too much.

Jesus falls.

The crowd takes a moment of depraved delight.

He struggles
and the crowd shouts,
annoyed and irritated
for the execution that awaits!

The guards force Jesus to get up.
He struggles and rises on weakened legs.
Jesus gives each of us hope when we are down.

Jesus,
remember me,
when you come into your Kingdom.

A woman stands by the side of a house.
She is dressed simply,
for just moments ago,
she was sitting at her cousin's table
making plans for the remainder
of the Passover celebrations.
Suddenly, there was shouting
and an array of hysterical people
at the doorway of her home.

The sentence hit like a bolt of thunder
　　that tore apart the morning calm:
　　　　"They have arrested Jesus!"

The color drained from her serene face
　　and the usual demeanor of peace and joy
　　　　was lined with fear and anxiety.

In seconds she regained her strength and
　　composure.
She raced out the door of her meager dwelling.
Mary, the wife of Clopas, and Mary of Magdala
　　took flight after her and within moments
　　　　were able to lessen her frantic racing.
She turned to these,
　　her friends
　　　　and faithful companions of her Son,
　　and she asked them
　　　　how this could have happened?
　　Just last night He was with
　　His faithful and intimate friends
　　　　celebrating the Passover.

"Miriam, He was betrayed by Judas,
　　and arrested by the Temple guards.
At this moment
　　He is standing before Pilate!"
The news of His arrest was a shock,
　　but this news struck a blow to her heart.
She could not even voice the words

which came to mind
for they numbed her very lips.

The streets were empty;
everyone had raced to the same place
and these three women were no exception:
the Praetorium,
the seat of Roman power,
authority and cruelty.

As the women neared the place of judgment
they found it to be a beehive of activity.
As they approached the compound,
the roar of the crowd was heard.
And it was frightening.

Mary's face was etched
with lines of horror, fear and terror
as the roar became a brutal chant:
"Crucify Him!
Crucify Him!
We have no king but Caesar!
Away with Him!"

Mary moved closer towards the screaming crowd
and through an opening in the mob
she saw Him and gasped.
It was indeed her Son...
hands bound,
face beaten and swollen,
His head covered in brutal thorns,

His body bloody
from the wounds He had incurred.
The blood had seeped through the tunic
that her own hands had woven for Him.

His head was bowed.
He was standing alone.
The crowd prevented her movement.
Had it not done so,
she would have leaped to the platform
and protected Him with her very self.

Above the din and noise of the crowd
she heard,
"Give us Barabbas!"
The words slashed at her ears.
She clutched her chest
and fell to the ground.
Those around her
were oblivious to her state.
And had her faithful companions not reached her
she would have been trampled by this mob,
so intent on blood,
so determined to carry out
the sentence of death.

She gazed
almost blankly
into the eyes of these faithful friends
and all she could say was:

"My Son, my Son.
   Why are they doing this to you?"
The women helped her to her feet.
   Her legs were unsteady
   and she clutched
      at their arms for support.
Tears streamed down her face.
   Her lips moved but made no sound.
A tragedy was unfolding before her eyes
   and her Son, her Child, was at its center.

In a blink of an eye,
   in just a brief moment,
   life had changed so radically
      and so painfully.

Jesus,
   remember me,
   when you come into your Kingdom.

Unseen and unnoticed
   angels sent from the High King of Heaven
      stood as invisible sentries
      guarding the mother of the Son.
An evening ago,
   they had assembled all over Israel
      to celebrate the power of Yahweh
      who had saved His people from Egypt.
But now, this morning,
   the power of darkness
   had enveloped His own city.

The mother,
    weeping,
    raised a silent prayer to Yahweh
        to save our Son.
Angels lifted this prayer to the throne,
    but on this day
        Heaven would be watching in silence.
Mary's memory flashed back
    to a time long ago,
    when the Man was a Babe,
    wrapped in swaddling clothes,
    nursed at her breast
    and slept peacefully in a manger.

Shepherds came with puzzled looks
    but bended knees,
    and wise men, stunning in their garments
    so richly arrayed,
    gave homage and gifts
    of wealth and praise.

Where were His followers?
    Why were they not here?
Her thoughts were harshly shocked
    and she was brought back
    to the present moment.
The crowd was roaring
    and again,
    in an opening in this sea of people,
    now a mob,

she saw Pilate wash his hands
while soldiers paraded Jesus,
    her precious Son,
        before this throng
and upon His shoulders place the crossbeam.
A parody of a parade
    began its grim march to the hill
        that they call Golgotha.
They shouted, "Take Him to Golgotha!"
And so, flanked by guards,
    they began a march
    from the judgment seat to the gate
    towards the hill they call the Skull
        to slay her Child,
        to nail Him to a tree
        and leave Him there to die.

The crowd moved forward
    and in a rush for a better view
    swept the mother into the cauldron
        of such misery and shame.

They laughed;
    she cried.
They spat at Him;
    she ached.
They cursed Him;
    she prayed.
They flung dirt and rocks;
    her heart was pierced and broken.

If only she could let Him know she was there,
   that He was not alone.
She followed behind,
   trying to reach Him,
   but the crowds kept mother and Son apart.

Suddenly, a hand grabbed her arm
   and steered the mother
      to a vacant street.
And, winding through the deserted path,
   she beat the crowd.
There, before her gaze,
   she and the Son she bore
      met eye to eye.

She heard no sound,
   felt no presence of the crowd.
And, in this moment of darkness,
   the light of these two souls met.

Blood was dripping down His face
   but that could not hide
      His glance and look.

Her heart raced.
   He saw her.
He knew He was not alone.
   She was there with Him,
      her Son, her Child.

Were she able
   she would have taken the cross

and carried it for Him.
But the soldiers moved Him forward.

He fell,
    the crossbeam crushing Him.
She fought the press of the crowd
    to rush to save Him,
        but she could not move.

A man steps forward and takes the beam;
    a woman rushes towards the Man,
        removes her veil
        and wipes His face.
Mary cries for mercy and compassion,
    the comfort she cannot give.
Others step forward.
    "Yahweh. Thank you. My prayer is answered!"

The heavenly escort that surrounds the mother
    leads her to the gate.
Her friends, behind,
    guide her through the portal.

The mother recalls thirty-three years ago,
    this same gate she had passed through
        with an Infant in her arms,
        riding on a donkey,
guided by her dear Joseph to the Temple
    to give thanks to Yahweh
        and to offer a sacrifice
        for this beautiful Child.

Joseph! She whispered his name
   and recalled his face.
Joseph! She called his name
   as she raised a silent prayer.
      "Please help us."

A soldier tries to stop her walk up that hill.
   She pushes past him.
   She will not be halted.
   Her place is near her Son.
She ignores his ranting and his curses.
Then she hears the tearing
   and turns to witness the tunic,
   woven by her hands,
   ripped from His bruised body.
Her precious and beloved Son
   so ugly now,
   so deformed
   for all the world to see.

Thrown to the wood,
   the hammer raised,
   the nail in place,
   the awful sound of metal to flesh to wood,
   the searing pain,
   the guttural cry He gave.…
She swoons and falls to the ground
   raising a wail and cry of grief.

The cross now raised,
   their eyes meet.

The gaze now will not be interrupted.

The mother rises and takes her place
    beneath that cross.
And on that fateful and fearful day
    she will keep watch.
The mother stands vigil and on guard.

Every ache He feels
    sears her body;
Every drop of blood that falls to the ground,
    she watches
        as His life slowly ebbs away.

His breathing is labored now.
    She breathes for Him.
Every breath He painfully draws,
    she breathes with Him.

She reaches for the tunic,
    but Roman hands wrestle it from her.
Not even His clothes can she hold.

The gaze between them is so intent,
    the desire of love so passionate.
He speaks.
    And to the one faithful disciple, He says,
        "Behold your mother."
    Then, to His mother,
        "Behold your son."
The end draws near.

The sky darkens,
   the rains begin to fall.
And a voice she has known for many years
   cries out: "All is finished!"
His head bows, His eyes close.

Jesus is dead!

The earth quakes
   but the mother does not feel it.
She moves to the cross,
   grasps its prisoner,
      moans and cries.
She releases Him with a kiss
   first to the wood
   and then on raised toes,
      she kisses with passion those bloody feet.

The nails are removed,
   the broken body is taken down.
And in the arms of His mother
He is placed for one last embrace.

The image of the cross,
   of the mother seated on that hill,
      the dead Son in her arms
         is imprinted on the human soul.
For on this day
   God gave His Son
      so we could live.
She kisses the brow so brutally wounded
   and still bloody,

the hands so ravaged by pain,
  now at peace.
Her cries are unrelenting.
She cannot let go.

They ease the body from her arms
  and with great reverence
  wrap its battered frame
  which moments earlier was filled
  with great pain and horror.
They move quickly to a borrowed tomb nearby,
  beneath the hill.

Mary sees where they lay the body
  and trembles when they roll a stone
  before the entrance of the tomb.
And, as she would not leave
  the foot of the cross,
she stands and waits outside
  this recently hewn tomb.

She tries to absorb
  the magnitude of what has transpired.
She sits now in stunned dismay and disbelief.
  She begins to hum a song.
It is a lullaby she often sang
  when Jesus was just a child.
Those who remain with her
  also wept, for they felt her pain.
    Her Son,
    her boy,

her treasure,
her life,
was dead.
And here she sat and sang a lullaby.

The city was quiet for many
who had witnessed the awful happenings
of this day.
They had fled to their homes
when they felt and experienced the quake
and the torrential rains that soaked the earth
and cooled the passions of the city.

Along the paths and byways
of this now eerily quiet city,
doors are closed and bolted.
But no locks could dispel
or keep out the unease and anxiety
that the events of this day had wrought.

In one home,
three women and a young man sit silently.
One – the mother – weeps.
Also a relative named Mary,
whose husband is Clopas,
stares blankly.
And a woman called Magdala
hides her face in her hands.
Her body heaves as she cries.
The young man called John

simply sits and stares.
His features are locked in grief.

Meanwhile,
    a distance from this scene,
    a father berates his daughter
    for placing herself in danger
    and doing so for a common criminal.
If the act itself was foolish enough,
    removing her veil in public was shameful.
Her father's displeasure hurt her deeply,
    but not enough
    to erase the look in the rabbi's eyes
    who, in the midst of His suffering,
    gave her a look of gratitude
        for her bold act of kindness.

Veronica held the blood-soaked veil in her hands
    realizing it was useless now.
        It could never be made clean.
And so, as she prepared to discard the veil,
    an odor of sweetness emanated from it.
And as she stretched the fabric
    she gasped
        for on the pale blue cloth
        there appeared an image of the Man
        in all His form, look and pain.
The woman smiled and hugged the cloth
        to her heart.
    And she whispered a silent prayer.

In a barely lit room a man sits weeping.
He is surrounded by nine
    frightened,
    weeping and grieving followers
    of the Master, now dead and buried.
Thoughts kept plaguing the big fisherman.

How could he have denied the One
        he called Lord?
    He thought and thought,
        he remembered and he cried.
    He wept for himself,
        for his failures
        and for his fears.
He looked at the others
    and cried again,
        for now they were all truly alone.
There was no Master to look to,
    no Lord who
        could calm the storms on the sea,
    to say nothing of those
        that raged in their hearts.
Jesus was no longer there to feed their hunger;
    no rabbi was there
        to teach them,
    no great Physician
        to reach out and heal them.

The more Peter recalled
    the more he wept

for having broken the Master's heart,
   the very heart that had loved him so.
He whispered, "Jesus, I love you.
   Master forgive me."
And he broke down again
   into heart-rending spasms of weeping.

Not everyone was at home on this strange night
   for in a tavern sat two men drinking.
Normally strangers to one another
   on this night they shared a common experience.
Their lives, normally so common and obscure,
   had intertwined on a road
   that led to a place called Calvary.
And both would find their names immortalized
   upon the pages of Scripture
      because one had met the Man Jesus
      and was set free
   and the other had carried His cross
      and become a new man.

Simon, a simple man,
   had just come in from the countryside
   and was pressed into service
   by the Roman guards.
He was told to carry a cross
   for a man condemned to die.

Embarrassed and mortified,
   he thought that others might think
   that it was he who was set to die.

"I am innocent.
   If I carry this wood,
   others will see and think
   that I am the criminal."
Resisting but frightened not to comply
   he bore the wood easily
   upon his strong and sturdy shoulders.

Simon will never forget
   the look in the rabbi's eyes.
In spite of the blood and the dirt,
   His eyes were gentle
   and expressed gratitude
   even for this stubborn act of kindness
   amidst the chaos of hatred and violence.
As he carried the wood
   his heart grew less resistant
   and the wood itself became no burden at all.

Arriving at Calvary and set to retreat,
   he heard the condemned Man say,
      "Father, forgive them."
These words touched the farmer deeply
   and, beneath the cross, he kept vigil –
   a silent witness to the death of this Man
      Who was treated so cruelly
      because He had dared to love.

He stood beside the Man's mother,
   a woman of courage and grace.

Neither spoke a word;
  rather both gazed upon the Man and prayed.
As Simon stood there,
  he lamented his reluctance
    to aid this dying Man.
Meanwhile, Jesus
    dying on the cross in great pain
  took a precious moment of His waning life
    and, with His eyes,
      expressed His heartfelt thanks
      for Simon's act
        of kindness and assistance
  while He made His way to the mount to die.

In this same tavern
  on this mournful night another man,
  Barabbas,
    was drinking heavy quantities of wine –
      ample measure, to be sure
      to dull his senses
    and to erase from his memory
      the picture of that Man condemned
  to carry the cross that was meant for him.
He knew the crowd had no love for him.
  But their anger and hatred
    lashed out at the One
    who was scourged and forlorn.
What trick was this of Pilate?

But, alas, this was no trick
  for on this Friday

Barabbas was not dead
but a free man.

Although his mind ached
from much too much wine,
Barabbas made a pledge.
And that was to find the ones who were followers
of the One now newly dead
and to discover what He said and did
to earn the wood
and to die as He did.

So, past Simon seated near him,
Barabbas enters the streets of the night
and seeks those they call Apostles
to learn about this Jesus
and to discover why *he* was set free
while the Man of mercy and miracles
became so despised and defiled.

Winding through the streets
he meets a stranger,
a man named John,
who recognized the just freed man.
As if moved by the Spirit,
John extends his hand
to the murderous zealot
and leads him to the place
where the others hide
so that he can experience
the grief and pain

and have his heart cleansed
and made whole again.

And so, from the barren cross,
the touch of the Master and Rabbi,
now wrapped in white
and in the quiet of the tomb so sealed,
reaches out of the darkness
and touches a soul:
"Behold, I make all things new!"

A restless Friday evening
turns into a Sabbath morning,
not with joy but with continued mourning
as the city awakens from its sleep,
the memory of yesterday far from gone.

On this Sabbath of the Passover
the people are sullen and apprehensive.
The events of Friday are still too fresh,
all too real.
The rabbi, this would-be Messiah is dead!

As the people go about their routine business
of Sabbath worship and Passover festival,
there was little joy.
Empty hearts recalled the tragedy
that had befallen
not just one family,
but the heart of the nation
whose very soul

is now swollen with blood
and poisoned with regret.

The Temple priests and scribes
were not so downcast
but were rather concerned about this problem
of Jesus and His followers.
"Post a guard," they demanded of Pilate,
"or else there will be a greater fraud
when the body is stolen
and resurrection rumors create a crisis
more severe than the Man himself."

And so Roman guards stand watch over the tomb
of a Man who was called a king
and now lies cold and stiff
on a slab of stone.

Mary of Magdala is unnerved
for the body of her Lord
was not properly prepared for burial.
Determined to make right
what was hastily done
she prompts John to aid her
to procure the necessary oils and perfumes
needed to minister to her Lord
one last time
and to see to it that Jesus
receives a proper burial
according to the Jewish Law.

She and John purchase aromatic spices
    and carry them back to the house.
They could not carry out their task
    on this special and sacred Sabbath.
And so the jars stand idle in the house
    as witnesses, silent and yet so bold.
Jesus is dead and alone in the tomb.

Mary, His mother,
    worn out with her crying
        acknowledges the preparations
        and is grateful
        for the courage of this woman
    so bent on doing the right thing for Jesus,
        her Son, who had been so wronged.

On the First Day of the Week

So, early before dawn,
   Mary awakens to begin her task.
She has the help of two others
   as they struggle to carry the jars
     to the garden.

Grief and mourning,
   tears of profound loss
   fall on each step
   that two days ago
   was a path of sorrows.

Daylight filters
   through the swift moving darkness and,
   as they arrive,
     morning has broken.

The area is empty.
   The guards are gone.
And much to the relief of the women
   the large stone is off the track
   and the entrance to the tomb is open.
Some reason for alarm!

Mary looks in and,
  adjusting her eyes to the dim light,
    expresses a reaction
    of fright and dismay.
The tomb is empty;
  the body is gone.

Two women fell,
  screaming in despair.
The morning is pierced by cries of disbelief.

Faithful Magdala,
  stumbling into the garden,
    breaks down and sobs.
Overwhelmed,
  she does not hear the footsteps
    of the One who approaches.
Near her,
  the Man, all aglow, approaches.
She hardly hears His voice
  as He calls her by her name.
Looking up through tears and sunlight
  she can hardly recognize
    Who stands before her
    and speaks her name.
Then, once again she hears her name
  and recognizes the voice.
It is Jesus –
  no dream, no magic.
    He stands right there.

Mystery and Love are wedded by a cross
and sealed with compassion and care.
She jumps to her feet
to embrace her Lord.
But He warns her, "Not yet!"
She is given a command:
to announce to the world,
"The Lord is risen!"
A new world awaits those with faith and hope,
for God has fulfilled
what was promised so long ago.
Humanity, this Sunday,
was embraced by God Who says,
"I love you; I offer you My Life!"

Down through the ages
we revel in this joyful news,
so filled with profound hope.
We delight in the story after story
of Peter and Paul,
of the disciples at Emmaus,
and even that of doubting Thomas
and so many others
who, for forty days,
lived in the presence
of the Risen Lord.
He gave a commission to them and to us:
"Preach the Good News
in the name of the Father,
and of the Son,

and of the Holy Spirit.
　Baptize all nations."
But nothing gives us so much courage
　as the words He gave us at the end:
　　"Be not afraid;
　　　I am with you always
　　　until the end of time."
But more comforting still
　are the words spoken to Thomas
　but meant for you and me:
　　"Blessed are those who have not seen
　　but have believed!"

ST PAULS

This book was produced by ST PAULS/Alba House, the Society of St. Paul, an international religious congregation of priests and brothers dedicated to serving the Church through the communications media.

For information regarding this and associated ministries of the Pauline Family of Congregations, write to the Vocation Director, Society of St. Paul, 2187 Victory Blvd., Staten Island, New York 10314-6603. Phone (718) 982-5709; or E-mail: vocation@stpauls.us or check our internet site, www.vocationoffice.org